D0099221

Waterborne

POETRY BY
LINDA GREGERSON

Fire in the Conservatory

The Woman Who Died in Her Sleep

Waterborne

Waterborne

LINDA GREGERSON

Houghton Mifflin Company   Boston New York 2002

For information about permission to reproduce selections from this book,
write to Permissions, Houghton Mifflin Company, 215 Park Avenue South,
New York, New York 10003.

Visit our Web site: www.houghtonmifflinbooks.com.

Library of Congress Cataloging-in-Publication Data is available.
ISBN 0-618-12010-6

Printed in the United States of America
KPT 10 9 8 7 6 5 4 3 2 1

Acknowledgments
My thanks to the editors of the publications in which these poems first appeared:
    The Atlantic Monthly: "Waterborne," "The Horses Run Back to Their Stalls." *Joe:* "Grammatical Mood." *The Kenyon Review:* "Cord," "Cranes on the Seashore." *New England Review:* "Pass Over," "Petrarchan." *Poetry:* "Noah's Wife," "Half Light," "Interior of the Oude Kerk, Delft, with Open Grave." *TriQuarterly:* "Maculate," "A History Play." *The Yale Review:* "Eyes Like Leeks."
    An earlier version of "The Day-Breaking If Not the Full Sun Shining on the Progresse of the Gospel in New-England" appeared as "Three Lists" in *The Yale Literary Magazine.* "Waterborne" was reprinted in *Voices from the Watershed: Living with the Huron River* and in *The Best American Poetry 2001.* "Eyes Like Leeks" and "Noah's Wife" were reprinted in *The New Bread Loaf Anthology of Contemporary American Poetry,* and "Grammatical Mood" and "Cord" were reprinted in *The Warren Wilson Poetry Anthology.* "An Offering" appeared, untitled, in *The Odes of Horace,* edited by J. D. McClatchy.
    I would also like to thank the Guggenheim Foundation and the University of Michigan (including the College of Literature, Science and the Arts and the Institute for the Humanities) for grants that enabled me to complete this book.

FOR KAREN

Contents

night studies . . . by reason of
the smallness of our candle
and its continual burning
— Francis Bacon, *Novum Organum*

Waterborne

Eyes Like Leeks

It had almost nothing to do with sex.
            The boy
        in his corset and farthingale, his head-

voice and his smooth-for-the-duration chin
            was not
        and never had been simply in our pay. Or

was it some lost logic the regional accent
            restores?
        A young Welsh actor may play a reluctant

laborer playing Thisby botching
            similes
        and stop our hearts with wonder. My young friend

—he's seven—touched his mother's face last night
            and said *It's*
        wet and, making the connection he has had

to learn by rote, *You're sad.*
            It's never
        not like this for him. *As if,*

the adolescents mouth wherever California spills
            its luminous
        vernacular. *As if,* until

the gesture holds, or passes. Let's just
                    say
        we'll live here for a while. O

habitus. O wall. O moon. For my young
                    friend
        it's never not some labored

simulacrum, every tone of voice, each
                    give, each
        take is wrested from an unrelenting social

dark. There's so much dark to go around (how
                    odd
        to be this and no other and, like all

the others, marked for death), it's a wonder
                    we pass
        for locals at all. Take Thisby for instance:

minutes ago she was fretting for lack of a beard
                    and now
        she weeps for a lover slain by a minute's

misreading. Reader, it's
                    sharp
        as the lion's tooth. Who takes

the weeping away now takes delight as well,
                    which feels
        for all the world like honest

work. They've never worked with mind before,
        the rich
      man says. But moonlight says, *With flesh.*

Noah's Wife

is doing her usual for comic relief.
                She doesn't
          see why she should get on the boat, etc.,

etc., while life as we know it hangs by a thread.
                Even God
         has had one or two great deadpan lines:

Who told you (this was back at the start—
                the teeth
         of the tautology had just snapped shut) *Who*

told you you were naked? The world
                was so new
         that death hadn't been till this minute

required. *What makes you think* (the
                ground
         withers under their feet) *we were told?*

The woman's disobedience is good for
                plot,
         as also for restoring plot to human

scale: three hundred cubits by fifty
                by what?
         What's that in inches exactly? Whereas

an obstinate wife is common coin.
                    In
          the beginning was nothing and then a flaw

in the nothing, a sort of mistake that amplified, the
                    nothing
          mistranscribed (it takes such discipline

to keep the prospect clean) and now the lion
                    whelps,
          the beetle rolls its ball of dung, and Noah

with no more than a primitive double-
                    entry audit
          is supposed to make it right.

We find the Creator in an awkward bind.
                    Washed back
          to oblivion? Think again. The housewife

at her laundry tub has got a better grip.
                    Which may
          be why we've tried to find her laughable,

she's such an unhappy reminder of what
                    understanding
          costs. Ask the boy who cannot, though

God knows he's tried, he swears
                    each bar
          of melting soap will be his last, who cannot

turn the water off when once he's turned it on.
His hands
are raw. His body seems like filth to him.

Who told you (the pharmacopoeia has
changed,
the malady's still the same) *Who told you*

you were food for worms?
What
makes you think (the furrow, the fruit)

I had to be told?

Cord

O.T.G. 1912–1994

Dearest, we filled up the woodroom
              this week,
        Karen and Steven and I and Peter's

truck. You would have been amused
              to see us in our
        woodsman's mode. It's your wood still.

You know those homely cruxes where the odd piece,
              split
        near the fork, for instance, has to be turned

till it's made to fit and another
              lame one
        found for the gap? Sap

just yesterday, smoke in the end, this
              clubfoot
        marking the meantime. I came

to one of them, one of the numberless
              justnesses
        a life of stacking wood affords (had you even

broken rhythm?) and for just that instant
              had you back.
        I know. I know. It wasn't the last, despite

the strangled heaving of your chest, despite
                    the rattled
          exhalation and the leavened, livid, meat-

borne smell, it wasn't the last till afterward, I've
                    made that
          my excuse. But Mother was sleeping not five

feet away, she'd scarcely slept in weeks, I could
                    have
          waked her. I (sweet darling, the morphine

under your tongue) am much (your quiet
                    hands)
          to blame. And when we had dismantled this last-

but-one of the provident stores you'd
                    left —
          a winter's worth of warmth in each —

and hauled it in, we split and stacked the new
                    oak Peter
          felled last spring. We took a day off in

between, we wrapped ourselves in virtue, we
                    can be
          good children yet. The gingkos

have come back from their near
                    poisoning, have
          I told you that? Our tenant's

remorseful, he's sworn off new insecticides. My
hour with you (one
breath, one more) was theft.

The Day-Breaking If Not the Full Sun Shining on the Progresse of the Gospel in New-England

I.

Oake, ashe, elme, beech, walnutt, chestnut,
        cedar, pine.
          Plummes, cherries, sassafrass, hempe. Widggins,

partridges (bigger in body as those of England), sanderlings,
        turkies,
          pheisants, quailes, bigger in body also, cranes,

fawcons, larks (the larks sing not), goshawkes, marlins
        great and small,
        a hummingbird small as a beetle,

owles, and all these are as nothing to the harvest
        of souls.
          Moose, porpentines. Lyons there are none. The

beares afraid of any man. Pilchers, lobsters, ironstones,
        lead
        (silver and gold by report), and yet

they see we covet them not theirs.

2.

Twelve grindstones,
two bundles of spades. We have not found

a journeyman printer willing to make the crossing.
Three bundles
of sawes. Chisels, axes, augers, hoes,

drawing knives, gimlets. A book on physick,
one
half measure of London treakell, one

and one-half books of pins for Mr. Eliots wife.
The ministers
exhort their flocks to a chearful and liberal

contribution. 1 oz. of safferon. Six dozen of
rackes
or spindells to spinn on the knee. Three bookes

against drunckennes, 3 dossen primers, a halfe
of them new,
a basket of pipin kernills for the Indians

to sett. Three bookes of Englands unthanckfulness.

3.

If but one parent
beleeve, what state are the children in? How

doth much sinne make grace abound?
          If so old
     a man as I repent, may I be saved?

When we come to beleeve, how many children
          doth God
     take with us? All? Only young ones? Or at

what age? What meaneth that, Let the Trees
          of the Wood
     rejoyce? What meaneth that, we cannot

serve two Masters? Can they in Heaven see us
          on Earth?
     Do they see and know each other? Shall I

know you? If a wicked man prayeth doth God accept,
          or what
     saies God? And how if a wicked man teacheth?

If God made hell in one of the six dayes, why
          made he hell
     before Adam had sinned? Doe not

the Englishmen spoile their soules, to say a thing
          cost them more
     then it did? Is it not all one as to steale?

What meaneth that, that the Master thanks not
          the servant
     for serving him? What meaneth that, that

we are not to covet our neighbor's house?
When all
the world shall be burnt up,

what will be then in the roome of it? What meaneth,
Ye
shall be my Jewells?

Maculate

I remember going door to door, it must
                        have been nineteen
            thirty-six and half the town was out of work,

we always had the Red Cross drive in March
                        (*consider*
            the lilies how they grow). The snowmelt

frozen hard again, and cinders on the shoveled
                        walks.
            I was wearing your grandmother's boots.

(*Consider the ravens, they have neither storehouse*
                        nor barn.)
            The grocer gave a nickel, I can see him yet,

some people had nothing at all.
                        And I came
            to Mrs. Exner's house (*no thief*

approacheth, neither moth). The woman
                        was so bent
            with arthritis, nearly hooped

when she walked up the street with her bucket and mop
                        (*not Solomon*
            in all his glory). The people

she cleaned for wouldn't keep a bucket in the house
                    (*nor*
        moth). She gave me three new dollar

bills, I'll never forget it, I wanted the earth
                to swallow me up.

                    2.

        Oilcloth on the kitchen table, linoleum

under his chair, and both of them an ugly hiero-
                    glyphic
            of yellow scorchmarks ringed with black.

My father must be tired, to let the ash
                    between
            his fingers and the still-lit butt-ends of his

days befoul the world around him so. Bone-
                    tired
            and all but hammered to his knees

with drink. (*Burnt offering I have not required.*)
                    The morning after
            the night he died (the undertaker's taillights

on the snow-packed drive), my mother sat just
                    there
            (*burnt offering I will not have*) and said

(*but only love*), I'm going to get a new kitchen floor.

3.

The raven is not
an unmixed consolation. What is manna

to the raven leaves a crust of blood
above
its beak (*a treasure which no moth*

corrupts). The freckled lily festers. The unspotted
lily drops
its trembling stamen in a smear of gold

(*laid up for thee*). And still it is no little
thing
to think we shall be eaten clean.

The Horses Run Back to Their Stalls

It's another sorry tale about class in America, I'm sure
            you're right,
                but you have to imagine how proud we were.

Your grandfather painted a banner that hung from Wascher's
            Pub
                to Dianis's Grocery across the street: Reigh Count,

Kentucky Derby Winner, 1928.
                And washtubs filled
                with French champagne. I was far too young

to be up at the stables myself, of course, it took
                me years
                to understand they must have meant in *bottles*

in the washtubs, with ice.
                His racing colors
                were yellow and black, like the yellow

cabs, which is how Mr. Hertz first made the money
                that built
                the barns that bred the horses, bred at last this perfect

horse, our hundred and thirty seconds of flat-out earth-
            borne bliss.
                He bought the Arlington Racetrack then, and Jens

got a job that for once in his life allowed him to pay
                    the mortgage
            and the doctors too, but he talked the loose way even

good men talk sometimes and old man Hertz
                    was obliged
            to let him go. It was August when the cab strike in

Chicago got so ugly. Somebody must have tipped
                    them off,
            since we learned later on that the Count

and the trainer who slept in his stall had been moved
                    to another
            barn. I'll never forget the morning after: ash

in the air all the way to town and the smell of those
                    poor animals,
            who'd never harmed a soul. There's a nursery

rhyme that goes like that, isn't there? Never
                    did us any
            harm. I think it's about tormenting a cat.

Double Portrait with American Flags

I.

Oscar will have told them that to hold
          the colors
      carelessly, to ever, for whatever

reason, trail them on the ground would be
          ungrateful
      in the last degree. And goodness is a kind

of curse, or God knows you'd think so, look at it
          forcing
      her shoulders straight. She will not know for years

why he won't look at her, already his not
          looking
      is the given world. The little one, the

redhead, squints directly at the lens. She's
          trouble
      and adored for it. How flatly, how off-

handedly, as though in a fit of overcorrection,
          the years
      will visit blight on her. So

slow jaws and so long a bruising. *This*
         is a country

where even a poor man has shoes to wear,

remember that. And one of them does.

2.

When Oscar
set sail from Oslofjord, his ship crossed the wake

of another approaching, upon whose deck one
might behold
the newly crowned King Haakon with the

infant Olaf on his arm. *The Danes again,*
said Oscar,
I left in disgust. But Mother always said it was

the shoes. How is it in a life beset with every
sort
of wretchedness that one thing, not the worst

to any outside gaze, will seem to have set
the pattern
in stone. The minister promised him shoes.

A boy who hadn't walked till he was five because
his mother
left him tied to the bed, who worked without

wages for twenty-four months on the promise
of confirmation
shoes — you see where the story goes, why

do you think they make such dreary movies in
        these Lutheran
     countries? Oscar till the day he died

would hear the sound of wooden clogs, a sound
        contrived
     to shame him, on the cold church floor.

3.

Clapboard housefronts, hand-held flags. A town
        inclined
     to march its children brightly

down the streets each May, from schoolyard
        to the willow-
     bordered public park, in deference to

the young men dead in ditches who had come
        to be
     in ditches, so the logic goes, in order that

the children might sit down to Sunday dinners
        in oblivion
     and peace. Scorn the civic argument, if scorn

you must, but do not scorn the dinners, they are
        doled out
     by a fickle hand. Had Oscar not seen misery

in every perfect plane of her face, he might
have seen
the way she looks just slightly to the

side, as though to spare him any open
asking. Thus
the dead will take up lodging in a daughter's

most instinctive act of thoughtfulness.
The living,
what can they do in this unrelenting

aftermath. Make holiday of
memory?

4.

Make penance of the air they breathe.

A chambermaid in Christiania's newly furbished Grand
Hotel — the merchant
class was doing well in 1876 — will have

been scouring stairs and emptying nightsoil long
before the sun
has ever shown its face, from dark

to dark, for five months out of every twelve:
the sun
at solstice barely ventures this far north

at all. And if she has no family, not counting
        the child,
          and no one else to help, she may be right

to think that tethered in his crib is all
        the safety
          she can give him. Not kerosene nor

coalstove shall destroy him, yet
        there must
          have been a fire, he did not freeze.

You who have cared for a child and changed
        its sodden
          clothes three times in a morning, consider

the odds: the leaden hours without her in
        the rented
          room, the transit of light on the floorboards,

the smell. And fifty years later this child
        of his own.
          At whom he will not look,

       5.

so faithfully her face recalls the
        lost one. His
          is one among countless such cases, they've used up

our will to imagine. No one
                arrested
         his family at midnight or stripped them of papers, no

malice at all was required here, always
                barring the shoes.
         But rather a portion of tenderness, look:

someone has ironed their dresses and carefully
                parted
         their hair, someone has painted the porch steps, and

the harshness to come forbears.

An Offering

(Horace 3.23)

Hold out your hands, girl, open
your palms to the moon, it's new,
      and new the grain and suckling
            pig you'll offer up with incense to

the gods. Do this with an open heart,
your vines will thrive, the pestilent
      scirocco will not wither them nor
            blight beset your corn, your lambs

will leap among the apple-burdened trees.
That creature grazing in the Alban
      Hills among the oak and ilex, he's
            already doomed, the neck

he bends to crop the grass is
destined for the ax. Leave axes
      to the priests, girl, and the lavish
            blood of full-grown sheep.

Crown your little deities with rosemary
and myrtle. A clean hand on the altar and
      a scattering of meal and salt
            are sweeter to the gods than gore.

Waterborne

The river is largely implicit here, but part
        of what
            becomes it runs from east to west beside

our acre of buckthorn and elm.
        (And part
            of that, which rather weighs on Steven's mind,

appears to have found its way to the basement. Water
        will outwit
            a wall.) It spawns real toads, our little

creek, and widens to a wetland just
        across
            the road, where shelter the newborn

fawns in May. So west among the trafficked fields,
        then south, then
            east, to join the ample Huron on its

curve beneath a one-lane bridge. This bridge
        lacks every
            grace but one, and that a sort of throwback

space for courteous digression:
        your turn,
            mine, no matter how late we are, even

the county engineers were forced to take their road
off plumb. It's heartening
to think a river makes some difference.

2.

Apart from all the difference in the world,
that is.
We found my uncle Gordon on the marsh

one day, surveying his new ditch and raining
innovative
curses on the DNR. That's Damn Near

Russia, since you ask. Apparently
my uncle
and the state had had a mild dispute, his

drainage scheme offending some considered
larger
view. His view was that the state could come

and plant the corn itself if it so loved
spring mud. The river
takes its own back, we can barely

reckon fast and slow. When Gordon was a boy
they used to load
the frozen river on a sledge here and

in August eat the heavenly reward — sweet
                    cream —
          of winter's work. A piece of moonlight saved

against the day, he thought. And this is where
                    the Muir boy
          drowned. And this is where I didn't.

                    3.

Turning of the season, and the counter-
                    turn
          from ever-longer darkness into light,

and look: the river lifts to its lover the sun
                    in eddying
          layers of mist as though

we hadn't irreparably fouled the planet
                    after all.
          My neighbor's favorite spot for bass is just

below the sign that makes his fishing
                    rod illegal,
          you might almost say the sign is half

the point. The vapors draft their languorous
                    excurses on
          a liquid page. Better than the moment is

the one it has in mind.

Half Light

(George Wishart)

I.

The broad way and the narrow, you see, in
        Upper
    Paleozoic shale, the argument having

come to this. If one side — call it *mine* — sets
        forth
    the virtues of method and rich

supply and, not so incidentally, of Rome and all
        its heirs,
    the other — *countermine* — shows

what a pickax and shovel can do with
        only the
    sound of the enemy's digging to

guide them. Vernacular testament, tables
        of stone. And
    here where the two converge and as

a consequence where many died the
        siege
    returned to stalemate. I shall never

think of *undermine* as merely of the mind
        again.

2.

Because the man would not keep

still, would preach against the errors of the
                    Church in
         Leith, in Montrose, wherever abatement

of the plague allowed. And furthermore
                    taught
         New Testament Greek. Was burned

at the stake on the first of March in 1546, you
                    may stand
         on the spot: unparalleled

view of northern coastline, sea, more rock.
                    The Cardinal
         said to have watched from the window where later

("a butcher") his body was hung. So two
                    to begin with: one
         in flames, the other unburied for seven

months, two versions of the one idea. Wishart's
                    friends, "the first
         reformed congregation in Scotland," held

the castle for nearly a year, their countermine
                    having saved
         the walls. The sea? Quite faithless. Would not

take sides. Indifferent to bombardment as to
        filth
    from the privies of righteousness, which

emptied on the cliffs below. The English
        reinforcements so
    long looked-for (this will not

surprise you) did not come.

3.

    You've got
    to be ready, my gardener said just moments

before his sod cutter severed the cable line.
        Referring not
    to lines so easily spliced but to his brother's

death at fifty, thus his own ("the family
        heart").
    Nor did he mean this loveliness is lost

on him: I've seen him with the lilies and
        the weeping
    larch. And look, he'll say. The motion

that begins among the crowns of oak and maple well
        before it turns
    to weather on the ground, he means, whereas

I'm lost unless the front has warranted
          some mention
     on the morning news. So second- or third-

hand, much as I've always lived on the earth. The
          difference
     is not nature — my gardener loves

his new machines — but something more elusive
          yet, some
     lightness of touch that by a common

paradox bespeaks the firmer grasp.
          George
     Wishart in St. Andrews would approve.

          4.

I think he would. The lurid
          light
     of martyrdom was always in this sense

an aberration, like the mounting of cannon atop
          a church. The
     church in question (1546 again) has

largely gone to grass and bare foundation stone,
          the choir
     and transepts unimpeded green. Which leaves

the quarrel where exactly? If the wall
> that held
> a window (fallen churches turn to open

excavations for the enterprising urban poor)
> has been removed
> to bolster up a cowshed here, a roadwork farther

west of town, in what sense can the window
> still be said
> to govern point of view? Nostalgia? Backward

longing not so much for death-by-proxy as
> for that
> which makes the dying incidental. Hence

our beggarly rapture at stark divides: the cliffs
> on one side, North
> Sea on the other, and the mutilated

body (there is nothing quite so good at this)
> for scale.

Pass Over

You point a camera at a kid, the kid
         will try
              to smile, he said. No matter part

of his mouth is missing, eyelid
         torn,
              the rest of his face such a mass

of infection and half-healed burns they'll
         never
              make it right again. You know

what the surgeon found in his scalp?
         Pencil lead.
              Six broken points of it, puncture wounds

some of them twelve months old. They figure
         the mother
              made him wear a ski mask for those

thousand-and-some-odd miles on the bus
         or why
              didn't somebody turn her in? The kid

is eight, the camera belongs to forensics, and
         he thinks

he's supposed to smile. Do the math.

If anyone here were in charge, my vote is scrap us
                    and start over.

2. PLAGUE OF FROGS

Indicator species is the phrase, I think.

Which means we pour our poisons in the streams
                    and swamps
            and these poor creatures grow an extra

leg or lingual tumors or a cell wall so
                    denatured
            that the larvae fail. In my new favorite

movie it begins as rain, a burst
                    of guts
            and mucus on the hero's car, the hero

such as he is, poor man, who's lost
                    his gun and now
            is lost himself before the windshield's slick

indictment, throat of frog, webbed foot
                    of frog, split
            belly sliding down the glass in red

and yellow closeup, thence to join
                    the carnage
            on the street, boot deep now, bred

of neither air nor water but of god's disgust
                    with humankind.
          Behold them, said the prophet, in

thine ovens and thy kneading troughs. And
                    then he said, Take,
          eat. This is the body you have made.

3. PLAGUE OF LOCUSTS

Because there's never enough. No, not
                    in this bright
          field of surfeit: milk rings on the phone bill, tracked-in

honey where the cats came through, lost
                    homework,
          last year's coggins on the tackroom floor.

My neighbor back in Somerville had only the
                    narrowest
          path to walk, from table to toilet, toilet

to bed, the rest was floor to ceiling with what normal
                    people throw
          away. I see how it comes to this. Never

enough of it battened down. I lose my pills, he said
                    to me once,
          they're rolling around on the floor somewhere.

The Parsis bring their dead, as Zoroaster
          is construed
             to have taught them, to Malabar Hill, where

when the world was well the birds
          restored them
             to simplicity in ninety minutes flat.

The birds are purpose-built for this, their scabrous
          faces bear
             a nearly paraphrastic kinship to the fetid

stuff they tunnel in. O who will come who will
          not choke?
             The birds cannot keep up.

4. HYSSOP, LAMB

Explain to me the writing on the doorposts,
          will you, now,
             while the angel gorges on them

and theirs, each that was first to open the
          matrix, first
             still matters in this first world,

that much I have seen and do in part
          acknowledge.
             Archived in the space behind the lintel

and its hasty script, a logic of division
          that has made
      the world articulate, a portal for each

fine discrimination of the covenanting
          mind.
      And heaven has its discards too, there's not

a book I know that tells me otherwise.
          I'm having
      trouble reading in this light though.

Was it something in the water, or before?

Narrow Flame

Dark still. Twelve degrees below freezing.
                    Tremor along
             the elegant, injured right front

leg of the gelding on the cross-ties. Kneeling
                    girl.
             The undersong of waters as she bathes

the leg in yet more cold. [tongue is broken]
                    [god to me]
             Her hair the color of winter wheat.

Petrarchan

1.

The dogs locked in the shed now
        so that Kit
           won't fall while she's alone: the mild

retriever, for whom time has spread
        its apron
           anyway; the young mixed-breed who cannot,

in her eagerness, track down the thrown
        enticement
           till she's stepped flat on it. Even

then. It can't be youth alone that makes us
        apt.
           The hush. And now — how odd — the hem

of rain: stippled lake disclosing weather nearly
        at our feet.
           I hadn't seen it coming.

2.

He wants, the children's father, something
        plain enough.
           May we . . . But Kit is old.

May we, when it stops raining, let them out?
    The girls . . .
   But Kit has heard a different question.

Yes she nods. *Yes good* he says. The
     eddies
   of benign misapprehension, braided

waters over rock. And Emma's interrogatory
     fingers
   through the yellow fur: is this

the spot? The hollow near the shoulder, the still-
     elastic hip: is
   this? The never-to-be-satisfied, the never-

named-till-touched-on crux. It hadn't once
     occurred to me
   that they were dead-on earnest, all

those bookish ones, about the flesh.

   3.

   Petrus,
   Peter, on which rock . . . *I've fallen*

twice, her knee is twice its normal size.
     So Kit's
   late-morning labor is to mind

the napping baby, whose eyelids with
        their sleep-
           flushed rims are Devon cream. Whose lily lips,

whose cowslip cheeks . . . Who wouldn't
        be confused
          by so much beauty in such little space?

Whose dreaming tongue and throat consult
        a missing breast.

4.

Of pieces then. Confessed.

The fieldstone barn, the sloping miles of fieldstone
        wall, albeit
          wrapped in chicken wire at several

tumbled junctures, mostly keep the silly
        sheep intact.
          Nor ever stooped to mortar: what the

stone-boats lacked, the mind
        supplied.
          Usable beauty's a patched-up

thing, Kit's knee does well to bend
        at all.
          Even the infant, so few

weeks old, has rubbed her silky head half bald
                    through turning
           to look at the — look! — at the new-again

world. The ratcheting herons return
                    to the nest,
           the rooster keeps faith with his hour. Wrong

                    5.

hour. And stony ground. *On Peter's* No
           I build
       my church. So, Woman, why these tears?

Did you think I meant you literally?
                    The late-
           summer foxglove and thistle are gone,

are all but gone, the juvenile heron
                    has fledged,
           and Emma loves another borrowed dog, for whose

dear weight she'll long when she's been long
                    let slip.
           What do you want that I can give?

What would you rather we die of?

Cranes on the Seashore

For Thomas Lynch

I.

Today, Tom, I followed the tractor ruts north
        along
        the edge of Damien's pasture. I missed all the

dung slicks but one. The calves did not judge me
        or, comely
        darlings, judged me benign. The ditches

and the token bits of barbed wire weren't, I like
        to think,
        intended to halt my trespass much more than they

did. The hedge-crowned chassis might have been one
        of my father's
        own. And then at the rise, Tom, the promised

North Atlantic, and I'm fixed. Salt cure for
        rheum. Rock
        cure for bureaucracy and blood-borne grudge.

The farmers on Orkney favored this time of year
        for pillage. Took
        to the sea just after the crops were in. Cleared

the mind.

2.

Megan
is not happy with her drawing of the

rock face. She has fastened on only this one pure
thing:
the light-shot swells of the tide do not move her,

the shattered interlacements and the rolling
greens,
she'd trade them all for the one right likeness

of ice-thrust slate. Megan is not by nature
ascetic — her
paper has smudged and the pencil lead snapped —

she's after proof the earth leaps too.

3.

At eight
o'clock on a Wednesday evening, eighteen

hundred seventy-four, one Jeremiah Dowling
(this
was June quite near the solstice, therefore

light) took aim "as he thought" at a pair of cranes.
The girls
in question, both of them in service at the

Leadmore farm, were washing skeins of new-spun
                    wool
            in the surf. And must have bloodied

the wool when they fell, but did not die,
                    or had not
            when the county paper went to press.

Of Mr. Dowling's youth and upright family
                    the writer
            cannot say enough (his obvious

promise, their moneyed remorse); we may thank
                    our different
            pieties we're less inclined to think these

help. We'd like to think our present dis-
                    positions
            bear more scrutiny, that girls

may be lovely as cranes and safe.

4.

            Behind
    the row of holiday villas, the hay

has started to rot in the fields. On the weather,
                    the hay
            and the holiday makers agree. But Damien's

calves have all been sound, and three to
        come,
    and Damien's father is glad for the extra (villas

need carpenters) work. It's like this at home now, the parts
        you sell in order
    to pay for the parts you keep, till my uncle

is told by the barman one day would he please
        not come in
    in his farm clothes, it puts off trade. A little

longer, barman, bid the locals then, A little
        while
    is all we'll take. I lied

about the calves, though; you can see the smallest
        Holstein's
    lame. Emma had thought he was simply less

greedy, so late did he turn toward the bucket of mash,
        and now
    she can hardly bear to look. God

keep us from the gun sight. Here is
        one
    for the landlord and one (we're almost

gone) for the road.

A History Play

Months later — I'd been cleaning
        my desk —
            these bits of gold foil spilled to the ground

a second time, five-petaled blossoms of public
        gaud
            unloosed from the folded playbill as in

August from the heavens at the Swan, Act
        Five,
            to mark the child Elizabeth's birth.

The old queen has been put aside (*I am not*
        such a truant as not
            to know), the new one's doomed (*the language*

I have lived in), the girlchild is herself
        a sign of grace
            withheld. But look at these sumptuous

velvets with their branchwork and encrusted
        pearl,
            you'd think the hand of death would be afraid

to strike. That's wrong. You'd think
        that death
            had held the needle and dispensed the worm-

wrought thread. The players will be wanting their late
        supper soon, while
   we — we two and our two girls —

set out across the footbridge on our way back
        home.
   The waterfowl will be asleep — they're sleeping

already — their willow-strewn and fecal
        island silent
   in the summer night. The past that for a moment

turned, backlit, thick
        with presence, as though
   leading to us somehow, in its very

inadvertence giving way to this
        slight stench
   beneath a moon-washed bridge, the past

that has a place for us will know us by
        our scattered
   wake. (*A strange tongue makes*) And morning

meanwhile yet to come (*my cause*
        more strange):
   the girls will have hot chocolate with their toast

and eggs. The play? (which we will talk about) Tenacious
        in its
   praise and fierce in its elisions. So

father, mother (older than the cast-off queen), two
girls: an open book.
And spilling from the binding, gold.

Interior of the Oude Kerk,
Delft, with Open Grave

Emanuel de Witte, 1653(?)

And you, friend, in a footnote, thanked
        for kindly
          inspecting the date "under magnification," who

are dead these twenty years. The author will have
        had some subtle
          point to make (diagonal recession of the

transept, fluent brushwork, more or less
        pronounced
          than versions by the same hand in another

year), the painting will have been remote
        (a small museum
          in a small midwestern town), and you,

well, you were graced with patience, you
        might well
          have taken pleasure in so formal, so

fastidious a task. And meanwhile this
        alembic
          light: the pillars in their radiant

stillness, honeyed vaulting, shadow
                plying blessed
        partiality, as if to say, the whole

view, yes, but not till you can bear it. Thus
                perspective,
        two-point, washed in milk. I do not

speak against that other beauty — lapis,
                vermeil, leaded
        glory with its saturating stain

of praise — but this, for me, for limpid
                intimation of
        the light to come, comes nearer, comes

as near as stone and pigment can be made
                to come.
        This church in Delft is something like

a village square: gossip, dogs, the woman frankly
                nursing, no one
        thinking she hasn't a right to be here,

the sexton at his homely labor, spade
                and shovel,
        pickax, broom. You wouldn't know,

to stand amidst this sociable
        vernacular,

how bitter the quarrel had been. And

see: the banished image makes a small
                    return. Red chalk.
        The children having found the too-

white pillar in the foreground too
                    approachable,
        they've remedied a too-consistent

doctrine with their brightest anthropomorphic
                    scrawls. How
        . . . what? How wry? How happy

of the painter to include so irrefutable an
                    instance of
        the will-to-speak-in-pictures, red

graffiti on the newly chastened canvas
                    of the church.
        And newly chastening: a four-by-eight-

foot flagstone has been lifted up on plinths
                    so the sexton
        may open the earth with his spade. Had he

thought to chase the children away,
                    he might
        have been spared some later work with soap

and brush. He doesn't think the dead
                will be much
        bothered in the meantime, though; his

country's built on water, he should know.

Chronic

They come in without their tablets, they don't
                    know what
            the tablets are for, I might as well practice

on horses and sheep. But look at these oxygen
                    saturations,
            we haven't had color like this all week.

(His voice unbroken balm.) We'll all be dead
                    before they'll invest
            in a new machine. (We were saved.) And what you've got

over there is worse. We serve a third of London,
                    right? And I
            am it: the whole of on-call cardiology. (You were

dying of *something*.) We were thick as flies where I interned
                    in Boston and half
            our patients got by without primary care.

(You were dying of something wrong with your heart.
                    You were
            not dying of everything all at once anymore.)

I remember one night shift I could not fathom
                    why no one

was there: Has some angel of respite pitched tent

over Boston? I thought to myself. At eleven fifty-
        eight exactly
      the first of them came through the door, then a flood,

including this man with his ten-year-old son, the son
        cyanotic
      from asthma. It had to be explained to me. The NBA—

is that what you call it?—the basketball finals had gone
        to a seventh
      game and then to overtime and nothing, not a nearly

severed thumb nor classic gallstone, had
        been able
      to peel these people away till the broadcast

was over. We had to admit the boy.

2.

      As when
      the light grows long again and casts its lambent

blessing on the lawn, as when
        the greens
      of middle distance, having banked their fires

in deference to the sun all day, resume
        their deep
      ascendancy . . . and all this time the change

I thought was what? was inward? was
                not purely
        inward but responsive to the chords

of sensibility somehow and therefore
                personal, this
        change has had a numbered explanation and a

name. *Purkinje* (Czech, and therefore
                mispronounced),
        Johannes, physiologist. As in

Purkinje fiber (atrioventricular),
                Purkinje
        cell (the cerebellum), and (not least)

Purkinje shift: coincidence of eye and
                world in
        favored wavelengths born of day's

decline. So *yellow* as the sun describes
                its circuit
        through the hours of busy striving, yellow

consciousness, and then the nascent shadow and the
                lengthening
        and then, as though we'd had the wit

to wish it, *green.* As when
                the one
        you love most in the world awakes

and sees that she must change her life.

3.

And so
there was something at last to be done, not

yet for the larger part, all that was and
had been
closing above your head, but for this nameable

portion in the chambered flesh: there was
history, there
were protocols, an undergrowth of Blue Cross Blue

Shield fetters and snares. And for a week we were
not fools.
Our garden in that city had a gate

and keys and gravel paths on which the children
could practice
being more than they were: canter,

lead change, supple-to-discipline halt and
bend. One
body with another in mind. And if

your longer sentence was a life in which
we had
no help to offer, still

something like the green mistake
          our rueful
          cardiologist would always link to Boston and

the hours of no new harm remained,
          had taken
          root. Or so I like to think now. I

am not so good with numbers as the man
          in Prague.

Grammatical Mood

There is, to her mind, only one.
                Or only
                one that's built to scale. Had they known

sooner. Had the only man to whom the CAT scan
                yielded
                so much detailed information not

been out of town that week. Had those few sticky
                platelets moved
                with just a shade more expedition through

the infant artery . . . The parallel life
                will not
                relent. But look, we may say to her, Look

at them tied to their breathing machines, they do not
                cry
                (because of the tubes you'll say, you're right, to you

the silence is dreadful). To you the vicious
                calculus
                abides no counter-argument: the oxygen

that supplements their unripe lungs destroys
                the retina,

leaving the twice-struck child in darkness. What

must they think of us, bringing them into a world
          like this?

        2.

      For want of an ion the synapse was lost.

For want of a synapse the circuit was lost.
          For want
      of a circuit, the kingdom, the child, the social

smile. And this is just one of the infinite means by which
          the world
      may turn aside. When my young daughter, whose

right hand and foot do not obey her, made us take
          off
      the training wheels, and rode and fell and pedaled

and fell through a week and a half of summer twilights
          and finally
      on her own traversed the block of breathing maples

and the shadowed street, I knew
          what it was like
      to fly. Sentiment softens the bone in its socket. Half

the gorgeous light show we attribute to the setting sun
          is atmospheric

trash. Joy is something else again, ask Megan

on her two bright wheels.

3.

To live
in the body (as if there were another

place). To graze among the azaleas (which are
poison
to humans, beloved by deer; not everything

the eye enjoys will sit benignly on the
tongue). It must
have been a head shot left her ear at that

frightening angle and the jaw all wrong,
so swollen
it's a wonder she can chew. Is that

where they aim, the good ones, when they're
sober? At
the head? At a doe? The DNR biologist is

saintly on the phone, though God knows he's not chiefly
paid
to salve the conscience (I have

bad dreams) of a gardening species stricken by
its own
encroachment. Fecundity starveth

the deer in the forest. It fouls the earth it
        feeds upon.
        Fecundity plants the suburban azalea, which

dies to keep the damaged deer in pain. I mean
        alive.

        4.

        For want of rain the corn was lost.

For want of a bank loan we plowed up the windbreak
        and burnt it
        (you must learn to think on a different scale, they told

us that). For want of a windbreak and rainfall
        and corn
        the topsoil rose on the wind and left. God's own

strict grammar (imperative mood). I meant
        to return
        to joy again. Just

give me a minute. Just look at the sky.

Notes

"EYES LIKE LEEKS":
This poem is for Daniel Evans, who played Francis Flute who played Thisby in *A Midsummer Night's Dream,* Stratford-upon-Avon, 1994. And also for Archie Brechin.

"THE DAY-BREAKING IF NOT THE FULL SUN SHINING
ON THE PROGRESSE OF THE GOSPEL IN NEW-ENGLAND":
This poem adapts passages, often widely scattered, from the following documents. Section 1: Thomas Morton's epistle "to his Majesties commissioners" on "the bewty of the Country with her naturall indowements," *New English Canaan,* London, 1632. Section 2: Several bills of lading accompanying goods shipped by the Society for the Propagation of the Gospel in New England (London) to its commissioners in Massachusetts, 1651–52. See William Kellaway, *The New England Company, 1649–1776.* Section 3: Questions propounded by Algonquian converts, the so-called "praying Indians," of Natick, Massachusetts, to their minister John Eliot and published as part of Eliot's correspondence in several promotional pamphlets for the New England mission, 1643–71.

"MACULATE":
Most of the italicized passages in this poem are adapted from Luke 12.

"THE HORSES RUN BACK TO THEIR STALLS":
This poem is dedicated to Jens Jensen, and to John D. Hertz, who gave him another job.

The nursery rhyme the speaker has in mind begins, "Ding dong bell / Pussy's in the well . . ." See *The Annotated Mother Goose.*

"DOUBLE PORTRAIT WITH AMERICAN FLAGS":
"So slow jaws . . .": This line is from Ben Jonson's *Sejanus.*

The city of Oslo was for three centuries (1624–1925) known as Christiania. Haakon VII (King of Norway, 1905–57) was Danish by birth.

"WATERBORNE":
DNR: in this context, and in section 3 of "Grammatical Mood," the initials stand for Department of Natural Resources.

"HALF LIGHT":
George Wishart (1513–1546), schoolmaster, preacher, Protestant martyr, was condemned for heresy and burned at the stake in the earliest years of the Scottish Reformation. His sermons are said to have converted John Knox. Cardinal David Beaton (1494–1546), Archbishop of St. Andrews, presided over the death of Wishart and was murdered in turn by a group of Wishart's followers, who proceeded to occupy the Archbishop's residence. The subterranean passage (the mine) dug by Catholic forces during the siege that followed was intended to cause the collapse of the castle walls. The subterranean passage dug by Protestant defenders from inside the castle (the countermine) foiled the attack. The castle fell in June of 1547, after French ships arrived to join the bombardment. Surviving defenders, including John Knox, were turned over to the French as galley slaves.

"PASS OVER":
The plagues of Egypt, and the painting of the doorposts with hyssop and lamb's blood, are described in Exodus 7–12.
The film referred to in section 2 is P. T. Anderson's *Magnolia.*

"NARROW FLAME":
The title and bracketed phrases are from Sappho, fragment 31.

"PETRARCHAN":

For puns on Peter, *petros,* rock, see Matthew 16:18. For puns on Petrarch, *petra,* rock, see, among dozens of other examples, poem 129 in Petrarch's *Rime sparse.* From Petrarch more broadly: we love what we can't have.

"A HISTORY PLAY":

The italicized lines are spoken by Katherine of Aragon in Shakespeare's *Henry VIII.*

"INTERIOR OF THE OUDE KERK, DELFT, WITH OPEN GRAVE":

The painting described is a fictional composite based on several paintings by Emanuel de Witte, Hendrick van Vliet, and Gerard Houckgeest. The footnote, however, is real. See Walter A. Liedtke, *Architectural Painting in Delft,* fn. 32, p. 86.

"CHRONIC":

This poem is for my sister. My thanks to Sara Blair for telling me about the Purkinje shift.